How Did I Get There?
The Power Of Choices

How Did I Get Here?

The Power of Choices

Patience Frisby

Blue Ink Media Solutions

How Did I Get Here? The Power of Choices

Copyright © 2024 by Patience Frisby. All rights reserved.

No part of this publication may be reproduced, distributed, or transmitted in any form or by any means, including photocopying, recording, or other electronic or mechanical methods, without the prior written permission of the author, except in the case of brief quotations embodied in critical reviews and certain other noncommercial uses permitted by copyright law.

Printed in the United States of America
ISBN 978-1-64133-950-6 (hc)
ISBN 978-1-64133-951-3 (sc)
ISBN 978-1-64133-952-0 (e)

2024.11.08

This book is printed on acid-free paper.

The contents of this work, including, but not limited to, the accuracy of events, people, and places depicted; opinions expressed; permission to use previously published materials included; and any advice given or actions advocated are solely the responsibility of the author, who assumes all liability for said work and indemnifies the publisher against any claims stemming from publication of the work.

Blue Ink Media Solutions
1111B S Governors Ave
STE 7582 Dover,
DE 19904

www.blueinkmediasolutions.com

Table of Contents

Foreword vii

~I'd Like To Thank~ ix

Introduction xi

1 My Story 1

2 Wisdom And Understanding 4

3 Choose Life Or Death 9

4 Disobedience Changes Your Destiny 15

5 A Vow To The Lord 21

6 Rebellion To God's Instruction 26

7 The Consecrated Things Of The Lord 32

8 Joseph: The Lord Was With Him 36

9 Forgiveness 40

10 Esther: Positioned At The Right Time 44

11 Gideon: Identity Crisis 51

Conclusion 57

FOREWORD

Fasten your seatbelt. Your entire life is about to change.

I know that seems like a gross overstatement, but if you are the action-taker that I believe you are, I am super excited about your future, and you should be too.

In this book you will finally get the answer to your most pressing question: How did I get here? And you will also find the strength to move forward. You are about to take a journey that will put everything that you have experienced in your life in its proper perspective. You will look at your past with fresh eyes, your future with unbridled optimism. And you are about to be uncomfortable, in a *good* way. Just like the author was the first day I met her.

Patience had the idea for this book for years but had not taken the necessary steps to bring her dream into reality. She was sidelined in the Land of Stuck. That is, until disruption came knocking at her door. God was the author of that disruption, and I was fortunate enough to go along for the ride.

As a multi-passionate entrepreneur who chases dreams for a living and inspires others to do the same, I have learned to embrace disruptions. Because more often than not, disruptions are catalysts to living our best lives. Just like they were for Joshua, Joseph, and Esther.

How Did I Get Here? can be that kind of catalyst for you if you let it—one that precedes an exciting new job assignment, a budding new relationship, lasting weight loss, or finally becoming financially free. The kind of catalyst that births big, bold, life-changing dreams.

Are you ready to live your best life?

Then grab a cup of coffee, get in a quiet corner, and crack open the pages of *How Did I Get Here?* This book is the real deal. It was written by someone who has walked a mile in your shoes and has the scars to prove it.

—*Tamara Jackson,*
Host of the Publishing Secrets podcast and Founder of ChristianAuthors.net.

~I'D LIKE TO THANK~

—Coach Tam (Tamara Jackson), for your endless encouragement, ideas, and support. There were days where I could not go on, and days I thought I could not write another thought for the book. You helped me through so much. Thank you!

—Funso Ore, for stepping in when I didn't think I would ever get this book edited. You are a great asset, and you work tirelessly to get things done. I appreciate you so much.

—My parents, for never stopping to believe in, love, and encourage me no matter how wild the idea. And to my siblings for being there and being yourselves—no matter what.

—My children, for endlessly listening to ideas, giving feedback, and just sitting peacefully without saying anything. I thank you.

—Rev. Young Irauafemi, for your first chapter edits. You allowed me to open up to others to get this book done. Thank you.

—Bishop MacJones for your prayers.

I would also like to thank everyone who gave words of encouragement, prayers, and feedback for this book.

INTRODUCTION

Have you ever thought of a situation, and in hindsight you realize you'd made the wrong decision?

We go through life making choice after choice without really thinking of the impact of those choices. Until the day things stop for one reason or another, and we look up and wonder how we got here.

That is the way my choices went. I wondered how my decisions felt so out of control. It became so much easier to go back and look at different pieces to figure out how I ended up there than to pay attention when making each choice, realizing each one has an effect. But now I have made sure the decisions I make are more intentional. Choices are not made haphazardly or without a lot of thought. They can no longer be made like that because each choice must lead to an intended destination. Some choices are difficult to make. For example, do you stay out late on a workday, or wait until the weekend? After making a choice, I hope for the best and pray everything will be pulled together at the last minute. What happens if things are not pulled together in time, or a major opportunity is missed because the only thing that mattered was having fun?

The destination will show the sum of all the choices that have been made. And then we figure out where to go from there.

Or we look at the available choices to make better ones. Not leaving so much to chance puts choices into your own hands.

~ 1 ~

MY STORY

One of the greatest gifts God gave mankind, after life and His Son, Jesus Christ, was the gift of choice.

The power of choice can have a positive or negative effect, and it can bring you to your destiny or away from it. Your choices are a guiding path that leads to your desires, based on what is chosen.

I thought about writing this book after hearing a sermon about the choices we make and how those choices affect our lives to an extent we don't even realize. When reflecting on life, it is easy to blame the lack of money, resources, and education, but looking at the choices we make can answer many questions.

In 2014, I was so happy because I finally got into law school. And by 2017, I felt so angry with God because, in the blink of an eye, it seemed my dream disappeared. It didn't happen that quickly, but it felt like it did.

I looked at my choices and how one bad decision can lead to another. I was accepted into law school, in Charlotte, North Carolina, so I relocated, while my children stayed back in Maryland. I missed them very much, but I felt this door had been opened for me for a reason.

The daily challenges of law school took all that I had— studying, ensuring I was prepared for classes every day, the fear of public speaking, being called upon to answer questions, and working on myself. Part of me was unsure if I belonged in law school. And self-doubt seemed to show itself at the wrong times.

At one difficult time, I had an issue with a classmate, someone in a study group. An assignment was due, and the person asked me to explain part of it.

Because I was finishing the assignment and preparing for the next day, I felt I had a limited time to answer. So I sent the person a copy of my completed assignment. The result of this choice was that I received a failing grade, and the other person was expelled.

I also realized, in order for me to stay in school, my writing needed a lot of work. Eventually, I didn't get the grades I needed, and the failed class (punishment for plagiarism) led to my academic dismissal.

During this time I was angry and blamed God for not protecting me from that person, not allowing me to pass writing, and not allowing me to complete school. I didn't realize I could have changed any part of the choices I made, and that led to my downfall. I wanted someone other than myself to blame.

It didn't stop there. I had an opportunity to appeal but did not put together an effective enough one to get back into school. So time passed, and I let it go. But the anger was still there.

I felt like a complete failure, and my actions began to show it. I felt that I could not get a decent job; I had let my family down, and I would never get anywhere in life. I eventually moved back to Maryland, with the same failure mentality, and once I was back around my children, they noticed the change. I was having a conversation with my daughter Jessica, and she told me I had changed. My walk with God had changed, and she needed me to alter my perspective. My reply was something like, "What if I don't?" and her mouth dropped. But at that point, I realized how angry I was—not at God but myself. I also realized that all the years of teaching and grooming Jessica, in spiritual principles and learning to trust God, could be potentially harmful. It could have her question not only me but God, and I did not want that.

I began looking at my choices and how they affected my relationship with God and my children. I didn't have to give my classmate a copy of my assignment, and I could have told him what to do. I took what I thought was the easy way out.

I could have worked on my writing before it was too late, but I didn't. I worked on it after failing the class. I should have had more confidence in myself because I knew what it took to get into law school. But my mind-set still told me I didn't belong there. These were my choices—which I had control of—and did nothing to help myself or set myself up for success.

The anger I had with God should have been with myself, from the time I was released from school. And either way, my anger should have turned into an action to set myself up for success, instead of bitterness.

I thank God Jessica is still walking with the Lord, and her relationship is even stronger than ever. And I thank God that she helped me see how negative I had become.

The power of my choices led me down a dark road. I didn't see the negativity until many of my choices led me to bitterness and anger.

But how we look at ourselves and what we think of ourselves is equally important in making decisions. Someone could have the desire to be a famous singer, but if he or she doesn't believe in the possibility to command the stage and wow the audience, that dream will never become a reality.

It will only remain a dream. If a person has low self-esteem and does not believe in him or herself, any encouragement will not be believed. Nor will they believe God loves them and has made them in His image. Therefore, the choices they make will be based on that negative feeling or low self-image.

In this book, I will discuss biblical characters and the choices they made. Much can be learned from their victories and mistakes. I will also explain why I picked the different Bible stories, and what I have learned from them.

~ 2 ~

WISDOM AND UNDERSTANDING

This chapter is about obedience. It is not about forsaking everything you want to do to be obedient to someone else. It is about your obedience to God. Had I been obedient in my choices when I was in law school, things might have been different.

As I look at the verses in this chapter, I think of what I truly did wrong and how I could have made it better for myself. Not only that, but I look back to see how some things, overall, could have been better had I had an understanding of obedience.

Growing up, I could have used some understanding of what obedience was. I was not always cooperative with my parents, and I would get into trouble; I'd made up my mind that I was or was not going to do something. There were times I paid the price for that. I would be sent to my room for hours at a time.

My father was in the military; he arrived home at around four o'clock from work. Dinner would be an hour later. Sometimes I did not want to finish my dinner, so I had to stay at the table until I finished my plate, while my sisters went back outside to play when they were done eating.

My parents would be watching TV or preparing things for work the following day. My mom would then return to the dining room around eight o'clock, wipe my plate off with a paper towel, and say, "Now go show your plate to your dad."

After that, I had to take a bath and go to bed. My siblings came in, talking about what a great time they had or the TV show they watched before bed. And I missed it all by having to sit at the table. So obedience has its benefits, and when you don't comply, you miss out on them.

Obedience will be what we read about in the story coming up—when it is followed and when it is not.

> Hear, ye children, the instruction of a father, and attend to know understanding. For I give you good doctrine, forsake ye not my law. For I was my father's son, tender and only beloved in the sight of my mother. He taught me also, and said unto me, Let thine heart retain my words; keep my commandments, and live.
>
> Get wisdom, get understanding; forget it not; neither decline from the words of my mouth (emphasis added). Forsake her not, and she shall preserve thee: love her, and she shall keep thee. Wisdom is the principal thing; therefore, get wisdom and, with all thy getting, get understanding. (Proverbs 4:1–7 NLT).

The scripture puts it this way: "Get wisdom and develop good judgment. Don't forget my words or turn away from them." Also, getting wisdom is the wisest thing you can do! And whatever else you do, develop good judgment.

You have a choice. The day this truth enters your spirit, you will never be the same. It is freeing. Once I realized this principle, it truly was freeing. I wished I had learned it earlier, but the blessing is that I have learned it.

The truth will allow you to make peace with the results of your choices. There are times when, once a decision is made, you will second guess it and wonder if it should have been different. You are left at a standstill, instead of moving forward. It can be liberating and regret-free, as long as you believe you are making good, godly choices.

What is wisdom without the understanding or the right judgment to effectively use it? When Moses died and God spoke to Joshua about what to do next, he had a choice: stay where the Israelites were for the last forty years, wandering around in the wilderness, in stagnation, or he could trust God and go into the Promised Land. Joshua went. The

Lord never told Joshua that there would not be challenges, but He said He would be with him.

> Now after the death of Moses the servant of the Lord it came to pass, that the Lord spake unto Joshua the son of Nun, Moses's minister, saying, Moses my servant is dead; now therefore arise, go over this Jordan, thou, and all these people, unto the land which I do give to them, even to the children of Israel. Every place that the sole of your foot shall tread upon, that have I given unto you, as I said unto Moses. From the wilderness and this Lebanon even unto the great river, the river Euphrates, all the land of the Hittites, and unto the great sea toward the going down of the sun, shall be your coast. There shall not any man be able to stand before thee all the days of thy life: as I was with Moses, so I will be with thee: I will not fail thee, nor forsake thee. Be strong and of a good courage: for unto this people shalt thou divide for an inheritance the land, which I swore unto their fathers to give them. (Joshua 1:1–6)

There are a few things worth highlighting about these verses. The Lord allowed them time to grieve the passing of Moses, but then it was time to move. Obedience in this situation was very important. When we lose a loved one, we want to reminisce in the memories and focus on what we will miss. The Lord allowed them to do that for thirty days; after that, it was time for business. Their obedience was key in getting the children of Israel to move.

The Lord wanted to assure Joshua that He was with him and that there was a blessing he was walking into by being obedient, not just for Joshua but for the people with him. In verse 5, the Lord tells Joshua that no man shall be able to try to war against him and win and that the Lord would be with him. In other words, you don't even have to fight these battles. Obey my Word, and I will take care of the rest. But then the Lord says He will not fail nor forsake Joshua. He heard it from the Lord Himself. What a great comfort to have. In the entire book of Joshua, you never read where Joshua doubted the Word given to him by the Lord.

Stagnation happens when we become complacent. There are places God wants us to pass through, but there could be a delay in us doing so. Taking the delay as a reason to stay indefinitely in our present state allows for complacency. When the choice is made to stay in your comfort zone, the next move is not so easy to see. Confusion takes place, and with confusion comes further stagnation.

Obedience is a choice I learned in my walk with Christ. Learning when to be the most obedient through difficult times shows maturity. And that is what Joshua had to learn as well. I have had many seasons where it would be easy to stay where I was and look at things I lost and things I thought I would never get back. Obedience is so much better than sitting around thinking about what you lost.

What happened is you missed the door because you became satisfied with getting spoon-fed and having your immediate needs met, but that was only to sustain you through the delay. When we become stagnant, God must open another door, but the things that were aligned for you (had you passed through the door the first time) may not be as clearly aligned the second time. Beginning to be comfortable in a place where you were only meant to pass through is a reckless decision because once you become stuck in the situation, it truly takes God to move His hand to get you out while working toward the second chance. Until that point, you must endure where you are, the place you are living, the job you go to, and even your resources because you missed the opportunity when it stood in front of you. Stay connected to the Lord so you can discern when it is time to go through the doors that are presently open.

Joshua saw all the miracles God did before the children of Israel. He witnessed the complaints and consequences, and he believed everything God told Moses and him. His choice was not to sit and wait for the next generation to step in to what God had for him. His choice was to enter the Promised Land.

Have you ever seen someone living vicariously through their children? Everything they didn't do is what they want for their children—to be the best player on the football team and make it to the NFL or to be a model, dancer, or singer and become famous. But when observing the person pushing so hard, this question comes to mind: What happened to your dreams? Why, even now, are you not working toward bringing any of your dreams to fruition? People give up on themselves in one way or another and decide their children must now fulfill their dream. Even if it's not the child's dream, they instill into the child the need to achieve it.

Sometimes this works, and the child becomes what the parent wants, but oftentimes the child rebels in such a way it destroys both their dreams, and neither generation can achieve anything. The good news with this type of situation is that both parent and child are still able to fulfill a dream in life if they simply change their mind-set and move to a goal or dream they want to achieve. The choice to become something better than what they believe they are right now is still their choice. Our obedience will help us get to that point.

Sometimes our biggest obstacles are ourselves, and it is vital to overcome those obstacles by changing how we look at situations and see ourselves.

~ 3 ~

CHOOSE LIFE OR DEATH

What does it mean to truly trust God? I have been asking myself this question.

The title of this chapter shows it is your choice what you will do. In Deuteronomy 30, we look at the difference between Lot and Abram. One trusted God in every part of his life, and the other only trusted God sometimes.

I have trusted people who let me down in one way or another, and there are times when it is hard for me to trust. But I have also not been such a good person that someone else could trust. I want to get better in that area.

When I first got married, I expected so much. I expected my husband to be the one person I could count on for intimacy, protection, love, and respect. I didn't realize that all that took time to build and grow, but I did come to understand that over time. And there were situations when I put all my trust into the marriage so that if anyone came against me, my husband would be there, and if anyone came against him, I would be there. Most of the time, it did not happen. Even going into years nine and ten, it was devastating to feel like I could not rely on that person time after time. My marriage did not last, but the lesson, though harsh, was learned. The experience taught me some things I had to unlearn, but it also taught me how to see a person's actions and learn to trust his actions and not just his words, no matter who it was.

But in trusting God, you can never go wrong. Jacob trusted everything God told him after Moses died. It must have been from watching everything God told Moses and what actions God took to prove what He was saying was true. No matter what, from the miracles in the wilderness to entering the Promised Land, God was faithful and did what He promised. We need to learn to trust God like that.

God said He would give Jacob everywhere he placed his foot and that He would never leave him. Even when all the other spies were telling a different story, Jacob believed what he saw and that he could take the land. That was his faith and trust in God.

Your choices are in your hands—not those of God or the devil. If things are working well, it is because of your godly choices, which determine whether things go well. Living a life of "anything goes" allows Satan to dump all kinds of things on us. There were things God told us to make a choice about, and we chose not to listen. Thereby, you pay the price for this indecision, and you cannot blame God.

God told man to choose life—that you and your children's children may have life.

> See, I have set before thee this day life and good, and death and evil; in that I command thee this day to love the Lord thy God, to walk in his ways, and to keep his commandments and his statutes and his judgments, that thou mayest live and multiple: and the Lord thy God shall bless thee in the land whither thou goest to possess it. But if the heart turn away, So that thou wilt not hear, but shalt be drawn away, and worship other gods, and serve them; I denounce unto you this day, that ye shall surely perish, and that ye shall not prolong your days upon the land, whither thou passest over Jordan to go to possess it. I call heaven and earth to record this day against you, that I have set before you life and death, blessing and cursing: therefore choose life, that both thou and thy seed may live. (Deuteronomy 30:15–19)

For a better understanding, here is another version: Now listen! Today I am giving you a choice between life and death, between prosperity and disaster.15 For I command you this day to love the

Lord your God and to keep his commands, decrees, and regulations by walking in his ways.

> If you do this, you will live and multiply, and the Lord your God will bless you and the land you are about to enter and occupy. But if your heart turns away and you refuse to listen, and if you are drawn away to serve and worship other gods, then I warn you now that you will certainly be destroyed. You will not live a long, good life in the land you are crossing the Jordan to occupy. Today I have given you the choice between life and death, between blessings and curses. Now I call on heaven and earth to witness the choice you make. Oh, that you would choose life so that you and your descendants might live! (Deuteronomy 3:15–19 NLT)

The New Living Translation gives plain English to what God is saying. He is telling man to choose to make the right decision. The paths are laid out before you. Once you make a choice, the decision, benefits, or consequences are on you. There is no reason to blame God for your choices. There is also a plea for people to make the right decision because God does not want to see anyone perish. But again, the decision is not in God's hands to make; it is in yours.

Now we are going to take a look at Lot. Lot was Abraham's nephew, but Lot's blessings never lasted as they should because of his choices. Lot was the relative who needed help with the messes he created, and Abraham was the one to help get him out of those messes. Lot decided to come with Abraham when God spoke to Abraham about leaving his father and mother and going to a land the Lord would give him. The blessing was pronounced on Abraham because of his faithfulness; he obeyed God in the things God asked him to do, but Lot chose to go with him. Lot's record with God was not the same as Abraham's, and therefore, Lot had times when he would be blessed based on his decisions and other times when he would not.

When Lot set out with Abraham, they reached their destination, and they found that the land was not big enough for all of Lot's and Abraham's cattle. They needed to separate. Abraham gave Lot the option to choose first where he would go. Lot looked at Jordan, saw that the plain was well watered, and decided to go in that direction.

In Genesis 17:5 God changes Abram's name to Abraham after his wife Sarai became pregnant. God also changes Abrah's wife name from Sarai to Sarah. By changing Abram's name, the Lord confirmed his promise to make Abraham the father of many nations. Now Abraham and his wife Sarah had the heir to fulfill this promise from God. Two things about this set of passages I want to point out : first, Abram was the older person and whom God pronounced the blessing upon. Abram should have picked first, but he allowed his nephew to pick. Second, sometimes, when you are looking for your next move, you cannot go by what you see in the physical.

Lot chooses to go by Jordan near Sodom, but God had not yet pronounced judgment on Sodom. The look of abundance here was deceitful. Lot's neighbors were full of evil—so much so that God pronounced judgment on two cities, Sodom and Gomorrah.

> And Abram went up out of Egypt, he, and his wife, and all that he had, and Lot with him, into the south. And Abram was very rich in cattle, in silver, and in gold. And he went on his journeys from the south even to Bethel, unto the place where his tent had been at the beginning, between Bethel and Hai; and Lot also, which went with Abram, hand flocks, and herds, and tents. And the land was not able to bear, that they might dwell together: for their substance was great, so that they could not dwell together. And there was a strife between the herdmen of Abram's cattle and the herdmen of Lot's cattle: and the Canaanite and the Perizzite dwelled then in the land. And Abram said unto Lot, Let there be no strife, I pray thee, between me and thee, and between my herdsmen and thy herdsman; for we be brethren. Is not the whole land before thee? Separate thyself, I pray thee, from me: if thou wilt take the left hand, then I will go to the right; or if thou depart to the right hand, then I will go to the left.
>
> Lot lifted his eyes, and beheld all the plain of Jordan, that it was well watered everywhere, before the Lord destroyed Sodom and Gomorrah, even as the garden of the Lord, like the land of Egypt, as thou comest unto Zoar. Lot chose all the plain of Jordan;

> and Lot journeyed east ... Abram dwelled in the land of Canaan, and Lot dwelled in the cities of the plain, and pitched his tent toward Sodom. (Genesis 13:1–12)

Sometimes looks can be deceiving. He chose the plain of Jordan next to Sodom, a city the Lord had chosen to destroy.

> And the Lord said unto Abram, after that Lot was separated from him, Lift up now thine eyes, and look from the place where thou art northward, and southward, and eastward, and westward: For all the land which thou seest, to thee will I give it, and to they see forever. And I will make thy seed as the dust of the earth: so that if a man can number the dust of the earth, then shall thy seed also be numbered. (Deuteronomy 13:14–16)

God's intention was always to bless Abram, but there are times in our lives that the only way God can release His blessing on us is to separate us from certain people. Once it was Abram and God, God told him all that was for him.

There are times you must endure what you have created to allow the separations from distractions (from people who do not have your best interests at heart and from fear), so you get down to just you and God. Once there, God will talk to you and tell you all He has for you. Your choice is to be willing to separate yourself so you are alone with the Lord.

God told Abram to choose where he was going because no matter where Abram went, he was to be blessed by God. In his heart he knew it, and he trusted God so much that wherever he ended up didn't matter.

Learning to trust God that much is a matter of going through tests and leaning on Him, especially when there is no one else you can lean on. Can we trust in the Lord that much?

Can we trust Him enough to say, "This is a difficult test, and I don't know where I'm going or where I will end up, but I will trust you"? There is a time in our lives when we need to move away from family to see if what has been instilled in us from birth—parents, school, college, and church—is enough to take that first step to achieve the life we've dreamed about.

Lot had to have immense trust in Abram. He called on him when he was in trouble, and Abram came. That is how God wants us to be in every area of our life. I want to be able to trust my spouse like that—and even more so the Lord Almighty. While it has taken time, I do trust God like that. It may not be in every area yet, but the trust is being built more and more every day. Every act of obedience is a step and test of faith to achieve a greater purpose. That is what making the right choices allows us to see over time. I may not have trusted how I needed to during my time at law school or immediately after, but the lesson has been learned.

~ 4 ~

DISOBEDIENCE CHANGES YOUR DESTINY

I included this story because it is about Joshua, who chose how he would trust and lead a people. Joshua had been with Moses to see how God guided and directed him. Joshua had confidence in God that He would be with him through everything and lead him through.

Confidence can be a powerful force. It is not arrogance but peace and acceptance in what you are saying and believing about a situation.

There have been times where my confidence sounded like arrogance, and I had to change how I presented it. I was pregnant with my fourth child, and we were at our first doctor's visit when the doctor examined me and said, "You are having a girl, and she will be born in December."

But I had prayed prior to the doctor's visit, and I had confirmation in my heart that I was having a boy and he would be born in November. I normally did not contradict doctors, but there are times you must speak what God shows you.

So I told the doctor, "I am having a boy, and he will be born in November."

Sure enough, after several months, my son was born on November 13, exactly as God said he would. It was a blessing to know I was truly hearing God in my life, and His word was true. I did not always keep trusting, and I had some bumps in the world with having that kind of confidence, but it was a blessing to know and remember the confidence placed in my heart at that time.

The children of Israel had finally exited Egypt and began their journey toward the Promised Land, in which God was performing miracles multiple times a day before their eyes. They got to the entrance of the Promised Land, and God instructed Moses to send spies into Canaan from the Desert of Paran. Each of the twelve tribes sent one person to go and explore the land of Canaan. They were given explicit instructions on why they were going and what they were looking for.

> When Moses sent them to explore Canaan, he told them, "Go through the Negev and then into the mountain region. See what the land is like and whether the people living there are strong or weak, few or many. Is the land they live in good or bad? Do their cities have walls around them or not? Is the soil rich or poor? Does the land have trees or not? Do your best to bring back some fruit from the land." (It was the season when grapes were beginning to ripen.) (Numbers 13:17–20)

The spies of the land were gone for forty days. They looked at and surveyed the land and the people, what their daily lives were like, and how they interacted with one another. They did as they were told in exploring the land. They cut off one bunch of grapes and put it on a pole, and two men had to carry it because it was that big. They also brought back pomegranates and figs. Looking at just the fruit, the land was truly abundant. The grapes must have been the size of grapefruit. For people living on manna from heaven, that must have looked like a welcome change and a feast. When you step into a new land and a new level, be prepared to change how you live and how you eat.

They also mentioned the location of each group and how their cities were structured.

> But the people who live there are strong, and the cities have walls and are very large. We even saw the descendants of Anak there. The Amalekites live in the

Negev. The Hittites, Jebusites, and Amorites live in the mountain region. And the Canaanites live along the coast of the Mediterranean Sea and all along the Jordan River. (Numbers 13:28–29)

I want to take a minute to explain how important it was that the spies saw where each group was located and how they were able to walk among the people in those cities, which helped them bring back a report. The spies discussed each location and a possible enemy and how their cities were fortified.

God told Moses that He would drive the people out of the land flowing with milk and honey. In driving out the people, Israel's children knew the location to create a strategy if they needed to go into battle. Each strategy would be different. For example, having walled cities, the Hittites, Jebusites, and Amorites lived in the mountains, and the Canaanites lived along the coast, representing a different type of fortress that required different strategies for different groups.

The spies had a great deal of confidence to go into a new land and walk around, observing the people and what they did, for forty days. They didn't talk about what they would do if someone confronted them, because it was never going to happen. How do you have that much confidence only to be so fearful that you lose the right to go back into that land and possess it?

But the biggest battle would be in the mind of the Israelites. Caleb encouraged Moses to attack so they could conquer it and take possession of the land. But the rest of the spies were saying they could not attack because the people were too strong.

"The land we traveled through and explored will devour anyone who goes to live there. All the people we saw weredescendants of Anak. Next to them, we felt like grasshoppers, and that's what they thought, too" (Numbers 13:33).

The rest of the spies agreed, and in their minds they were already defeated, and they had only explored the land. Their mind-set was interesting, because when they explored the land and no one bothered them, they were able to walk around for days without conflict or any negative encounter, but they reported that the people were too strong for them. They were already defeated.

Fear set in so strongly that they could not see themselves moving forward in any way, and they defeated themselves without having an enemy to fight. How many times do we do that in our lives? We are about to get blessed, and we look at the circumstances and defeat ourselves. If they only had enough faith to step into the new land, they would have been blessed.

That night the people lifted their voices against Moses and God. Their fear took on many different words and scenarios. They complained to Moses and Aaron that they should have died in Egypt instead of in the desert. They asked why the Lord was bringing them into a land for them to die. Moses and Aaron bowed and prayed and tore their clothes. Even Joshua and Caleb were praying and tearing their clothes in despair because they saw the potential in the land they just explored. The complaints went on so long that after a while, Moses went to God with a complaint: "But Moses said to the Lord, 'What if the Egyptians hear about it? (You used your power to take these people away from them)'" (Numbers 14:13).

Can you imagine God's reaction to that? If I were God, I would be so angry at that statement because it was not the Egyptians who saved them, nor were they the ones who hardened Pharaoh's heart for the Israelites to leave Egypt and go through all they did to have Pharaoh and his army die in the Red Sea. Not only that, God gave the Israelites miracle after miracle, day after day, only for them to turn around and ask if the Egyptians heard about their new issue (which was not an actual issue but in their minds).

God continues to listen to what Moses is saying, but then when Moses finishes, in Numbers 14:32, God says, "But as for you, your carcasses, they shall fall in this wilderness."

Can you imagine that judgment upon your life? That is why Moses never crossed into Canaan, into the land flowing with milk and honey, but Caleb did.

It is a sad pronouncement when your own mouth makes you lose out on your blessing, but that is what happened to Moses. It seems Moses allowed the fear of others to change his mind from what he saw, from what the Promised Land would look like.

The God-confidence I mentioned in the story earlier was not something I realized I had until it came out. Joshua had God-confidence when he led the children of Israel into the Promised Land. It is not something you second-guess; you just push forward.

So what if the result does not look like what we thought it should? Is that a reason to question God? Should you allow your fear to set in so much that after talking to God, you doubt and question Him and end up never getting to see the Promised Land? Can you imagine wanting something so much that you wait on God for the promise, get to the promise, and don't believe it is for you? I can't imagine going through all that or allowing a choice of doubt to turn me away. Truly, hope deferred makes the heart sad (Proverbs 13:12). But to finally see what you have been hoping for and willingly lose it seems like the worst position to put yourself in because the rest of your days, your thought will be, *It could have been mine if only I had trusted God.* It cost a promise of God to be seen but not enjoyed by Moses and ultimately leading only the people younger than twenty to step into the Promised Land.

The power of your choices may not seem like much, but if you trust God, always remember that His thoughts are higher than ours (Isaiah 55:8). What we think of as just another house, another car, or travel from one state to another is much more a part of God's plan for us. The steps we take lead us through, at times, difficult paths, and we can't look at "just another house"

as our end result. What God has planned is much bigger than what you can think or imagine for yourself.

To question the downward spiral was when the doubt came into Moses's mind, and he began to question God. What if the Egyptians hear? What if they hear that you are about to enter the land God promised you? That you are stepping into your season and life of prosperity? By prosperity, I mean a life of rest, where you don't have to fight, toil, or struggle anymore.

I wanted that confidence that my choices would lead to where God wanted me to go, but my decisions were not always in line with God's will during law school. Now that I know where I lost focus, I can reset my choices and move forward.

Instead, Moses's mind was on, *What if the Egyptians hear and come after us?* He said a lot more to God after that and lost his entrance into the Promised Land. Once the mind goes to a place of negativity, the thoughts come one after the other. What if Moses had fought those thoughts and waited to see what God would do? What if he kept quiet and went into the Promised Land?

The choices Moses made cost him dearly, but his seed inherited the land flowing with milk and honey. What are you potentially giving up because you're making choices based on what you think instead of what the Lord is telling you?

~ 5 ~

A VOW TO THE LORD

Making a vow seems to be taken lightly. Marriage and divorce are common practices in our churches today. But what if someone's life depended on it? The vow in this chapter had someone's life hanging in the balance; it was handled well.

My vows of marriage are no longer, but there are times I wonder if we had this type of reaction to the vow, if we were steadfast in our vows and would do all that was necessary to keep them. This story shows that when you are raising your children a certain way, once on their own to make choices, they will do what you have instilled in them. I chose this story because of the confidence Jephthah had in how he raised his family, and he knew they would follow instructions, having that confidence even being away at war.

Raising a family is not easy, and being a single parent may not be a desired task. But the process of raising your children still needs to be done. During the teenage years, children test boundaries like never before because they are looking for their independence. They are also trying to find out if they can make it on their own. I used to tell my children to go away to college because you get to know who you and what you're made of there. In college, you have little money, and you have to make it last. If you get a job, you have to balance school and work while still learning how to deal with your friends and social life with your new independence.

More importantly, that is when the value your parents taught you come into play more often than you think. You are constantly tested in this area because of independence but also because of the choices and temptations that will constantly come into play and come with consequences you may not be aware of.

What would you do if a choice one of your parents made had consequences that affected you? Would you honor the choice or run away? And what would you do if you found out the choice was not intentional, but your parents knew no matter what that you would honor it because that was how you were raised? Would it be a hard choice for you?

Making a vow to God is your choice. So is keeping that vow.

Making a vow to God is between you and the Lord. God will always hold up His end of a vow, but He requires that you keep your part as well. It seems people are carefree when making a vow to God. A person may want to get through something, so he or she makes a vow to God that "if you get me through this, I will go to church every Sunday." When making the vow, the person has every intention to keep it, but then sometimes breaking the vow to the Lord is worse than if you had never made the vow in the first place. Sometimes making the vow puts you in a difficult position.

Let's look at Jephthah and his vow to the Lord. We need to understand who Jephthah is and find out how he was a great blessing and a testament to his character.

> Now Jephthah the Gilead was a mighty man of valor, and he was the son of a harlot: and Gilead begat Jephthah. And Gilead's wife bare him a son; and his wife's sons grew up, and they thrust out Jephthah, and said unto him Thou shalt not inherit in our father's house; for thou art the son of a strange woman. Then Jephthah fled from his brethren, and dwelt in the land of Tob: and there were gathered vain men to Jephthah, and went out with him. And it came to pass the in process of time, that the children of Ammon made war against Israel, and it was so, that when the children of Ammon made war against Israel, the elders of Gilead went to fetch Jephthah out of the land of Tob: and they said unto Jephthah, Come, and be our captain, that we may fight with the children of Ammon. (Judges 11:1–6)

How Did I Get Here? The Power of Choices

This set of scriptures gives you an idea of how Jephthah grew up. He was the son of a prostitute and a man who already had a wife and many sons. His father took Jephthah in, but after some time, his stepbrothers threw him out because they did not want to share their father's inheritance with Jephthah.

Tob is where Jephthah ran to and is where the leaders of Gilead went to find him when the Ammonites made war against Israel to make him their captain.

His response was not immediate:

> And Jephthah said unto the elders of Gilead, Did not ye hate me, and expel me out of my father's house? And why are ye come unto me now when ye are in distress? And Jephthah said unto the elders of Gilead, If ye bring me home again to fight against the children of Ammon, and the Lord deliver them before me, shall I be your head? And the leaders of Gilead said unto Jephthah, The Lord be witness between us, if we do not so according to the words. Then Jephthah went with the elders of Gilead, and the people made him head and captain over them: and Jephthah uttered all his words before the Lord in Mizpeh. (Judges 11:7–10)

The leaders contributed to him being thrown out of the house by his stepbrothers. Now the leaders asked Jephthah to help fight the Amorites—and not only help fight but to be captain. Jephthah agreed to be captain.

The vow was made to the Lord because Jephthah wanted to have a successful outcome of the war and to ensure the Israelites were victorious.

"And Jephthah vowed a vow to the Lord, and said, if you will indeed give the children of Ammon into my hand. Then it shall be that whatever comes out from the doors of my house to meet me when I return in peace from the children of Ammon, surely it shall belong to the Lord, or I will offer it up instead of a burnt sacrifice" (Judges 11:30–31).

The Israelites were victorious in their battle with Ammon and other battles they fought. So Jephthah returned home to Mizpeh. The first person through the door when Jephthah returned was his only child. "And Jephthah came to Mizpeh unto his house, and behold his daughter came out to meet him with timbrels and with dances: and she was his only child; beside her, he had neither son nor daughter" (Judges 11:34).

Jephthah probably thought one of his servants would come out of the door first to greet him. His daughter was still a virgin. He tore his clothes and was quite upset. Jephthah having to keep this vow meant he would have no heir and no one to carry on the family name or heritage, which was a disgrace in those days.

Once Jephthah told his daughter the vow he made before the Lord, she had a request of her father. She said, "Let this thing be done for me. Let me alone two months, so that I may go up and down the mountains and weep for my virginity, I and my companions" (Judges 11:38).

What a mature attitude about becoming a sacrifice and not feeling sorry for herself because of the vow her father made. I have researched and discovered that the vow meant one of two things to Jephthah's daughter. The first would be for her father to kill her after those two months, to lay her on an altar as Abraham did Isaac; or second, she was to be consecrated to the Lord for the rest of her life, never to marry or have children.

She was a virgin consecrated for the Lord. She asked to go up and down the mountain to mourn with her companions for her virginity because she would never lose it. Her sacrifice was to be a perpetual virgin in the Lord's house, serving Him for the rest of her life. Judges 11 reads, "And she knew no man."

Jephthah kept his vow to the Lord, and in Hebrew 11:32, he is mentioned as having great faith. Sometimes our choices affect more than just us.

What would happen if Jephthah's daughter refused to fulfill the vow to be complete? Would it still have been complete in God's eyes?

Jephthah had to know those of his household would keep that type of vow and it would be fulfilled. He had to know that his daughter, his wife, and his servants would be obedient no matter the cost.

If we think of our families and make that type of vow today to God, would it be fulfilled? The thought may be, oh, it is a different time, but for some things, it's not. For faith and obedience, it was not for a man to know what he has instilled in the life of his household that what is asked of them by him will be trusted. What is instilled is not fear but respect.

Jephthah had great faith in God. His beginnings were hard, and there was no telling how his story would end. But despite the rough start, he finished strong—strong enough to be mentioned in the New Testament as a man of faith. His choices of trusting in God earned him much respect from his family, the men who served under him, and God.

As a parent, you want your children to do what you have instilled in them. This story shows exactly that.

~ 6 ~

REBELLION TO GOD'S INSTRUCTION

Receiving instructions and following them is important. But what happens when instructions are deliberately not followed? Have you ever received an instruction from your parents or any person in a position of authority and flat-out stated you were not going to do it? That is what this chapter is about.

When I was about twelve, my dad told me to do something, and I didn't want to do it, so I said no. Well, praise God I lived to tell about it, but I received a spanking that day and was sent to my room. What I get now that I didn't get then is that I was disrespectful. I remember that situation like it was yesterday. The lesson it taught was important. People who are looking out for your good deserve your respect. Just because you may not know the reason does not mean you should not do what is requested. How much more honor and respect for God?

Jonah is a popular children's story in the Bible because he refused to follow the Lord's instructions. Where he ended up may not be as comfortable or desirable as the story seems—in the belly of a great fish. Thinking about the contents of the stomach of a great fish even for one day makes my stomach turn. Jonah was there three days before he repented and the great fish spewed him out.

Jonah didn't want to do what the Lord instructed not once but twice. Jonah wanted the Lord to destroy the people of Nineveh because

How Did I Get Here? The Power of Choices

he thought judgment should be upon them. He didn't want them to have the opportunity to repent and change.

How many people in our lives would no longer be living if we were to take judgment into our own hands? Thank you, Lord, for providing judgment.

> Now the word of the Lord came unto Jonah the son of Amittai, saying, "Arise, go to Nineveh, that great city, and cry against it; for their wickedness is come up before me." But Jonah rose up to flee unto Tarshish from the presence of the Lord, and went down to Joppa. He found a ship going to Tarshish: so he paid the fare thereof, and went down into it, to go with them unto Tarshish from the presence of the Lord. (Jonah 1:1–3)

The Lord spoke directly to Jonah to do something He wanted done. Jonah heard the Lord and went in a completely different direction. Next, Jonah went on the ship to Tarshish to get away from the presence of the Lord. It would not have mattered where Jonah went; he could never escape the presence of the Lord. The Lord sees and knows all.

> But the Lord sent out a great wind into the sea, and there was a mighty tempest in the sea, so that the ship was like to be broken. Then the mariners were afraid, and cried every man unto his god, and cast forth the wares that were in the ship into the sea, to lighten it of them. But Jonah was gone down into the sides of the ship; and he lay, and was fast asleep. (Jonah1:4–5)

Jonah was not only disobedient, but in what seemed like the worst storm, these mariners could not imagine Jonah was sleeping and didn't notice the storm.

Many of us are stubborn when we are disobedient; we do not notice the storm the Lord sent to wake us up—not from a natural sleep but from the foolish direction we have taken that is leading us away from the Lord. There are times we all need a wakeup call from the Lord. Also, these mariners threw their wares into the sea to lighten the load, meaning they lost whatever they were going to sell or have delivered to make money for their journey in the first place.

In the course of our disobedience, how much do we lose or allow others to lose because we decide not to see what is in front of our faces? Or maybe we become blind because the Lord must open our eyes again to see the value of a thing.

> So the shipmaster came to him, and said unto him, What meanest thou, O sleeper? Arise, call upon they God, if so be that God will think upon us, that we perish not. And they said everyone to his fellow, Come, and let us cast lots, that we may know for whose cause this evil is upon us. So they cast lots, and the lot fell upon Jonah. Then said they unto him, Tell us, we pray thee, for whose cause this evil is upon us? What is thine occupation? And whence comest thou? What is their country? And if what people art thou? (Jonah 1:-5–8)

Jonah's fellow shipmates did not do anything about him, but now they needed to know because of the great storm that was upon them.

> And he said unto them, I am a Hebrew; and I fear the Lord, the God of heaven, which hath made the sea and the dry land. Then were the men exceedingly afraid, and said unto him. Why hast thou done this: For the men knew that he fled from the presence of the Lord, because he had told them.
>
> Then said they to him, "What shall we do unto thee, that the sea may be calm unto us? For the sea wrought, and was tempestuous. And he said unto them, Take me up, and cast me forth into the sea; so shall the sea be calm upon you: for I know that for my sake this great tempest is upon you.
>
> Nevertheless, the men rowed hard to bring it to the land; but they could not: for the sea wrought, and was tempestuous against them. Wherefore they cried unto the Lord, and said, we beseech thee, O Lord, we

How Did I Get Here? The Power of Choices

beseech thee, let us not perish for this man's life, and lay not upon us innocent blood: for thou, O Lord, hast done as it pleased thee. So they took up Jonah, and cast him forth into the sea: and the sea ceased from her raging. Then the men feared the Lord exceedingly, and offered a sacrifice unto the Lord, and made vows. Now the Lord had prepared a great fish to swallow up Jonah. And Jonah was in the belly of the fish for three days and three nights (Jonah 1:13-17 KJV)

There is so much in these passages, including humor. After Jonah's shipmates ask all these questions, Jonah says he is a child of God and the cause of the storm. They ask Jonah what they should do to him, and he tells them to throw him overboard. Jonah knows all this is his fault, so to calm the sea, that is their only option. Also, the men seem to think it would be sudden death for Jonah, so they don't immediately do it. They rowed as fast as they could to get to land, but it doesn't work because the tempest is from God, so no matter how much they try to avoid the situation, it will not work. The men did what Jonah asked and threw him into the sea, and the storm stopped.

I can imagine the dumbfounded looks on the men's faces because it could only be from God. I have often wondered what the men's faces were like at seeing the great fish jump up to swallow Jonah at the same time Jonah was thrown overboard. That is another moment where you just can't believe what happened unless you were there to witness it. Nevertheless, Jonah was in the great fish for three days and three nights. While there he prays to the Lord. In all this time, he could have died, but the Lord showed mercy and saved him. The Lord's mercy triumphed over judgment and showed His faithfulness to Jonah, who was grateful to God for His salvation. After that prayer, the Lord spoke to the fish and it vomited up Jonah on dry land.

This is not the end of the story because Jonah still has a mission to complete. "And the word of the Lord came unto Jonah the second time, saying, Arise, go unto Nineveh, that great city, and preach unto it the preaching that I bid thee" (Jonah 3:1–2).

What I find interesting is that God tells Jonah to go again, as if the events of the previous chapter didn't happen. God tells him to go to Nineveh and do what He said.

That was another choice Jonah had to make. People look at him being in the belly as just a place God sent him for a few days, but in Jonah 2, it was not an easy experience for Jonah to go through. The waves and the floods must have been continuous because large fish eat a lot, and the way they do it is to open their mouths and swim into a school of fish, catching everything in its path. That includes water, seaweed, plants, and the smaller fish. Imagine enduring that several times a day! Jonah 3:3 says, "So Jonah arose, and went unto Nineveh, according to the work of the Lord."

Jonah went and proclaimed a fast for Nineveh to repent, and Nineveh did just that. God saw their works. They turned from their evil ways, and God repented of the punishment He was going to do to that city. Jonah was not happy with this because he wanted Nineveh to be punished. Jonah went east of the city and made a booth and sat under a shadow. The Lord allowed a plant to grow over him to provide shade, but Jonah continued to complain, so the Lord prepared a worm to eat the plant. The Lord asked Jonah if it were better for the plant to perish in a night and for him not to have spared Nineveh, where there were thousands.

Jonah said in Jonah 4:3, "For It is better for me to die than to live."

After Nineveh repented, Jonah was not happy; all the talking God did with Jonah did not change his mind.

Are we angry when God saves someone we think should have been destroyed? We must repent of this attitude, ask for forgiveness, and let God be the judge, lest we end up as Jonah. I have always looked at the story of Jonah as a children's story. It is told in many children's Sunday school classrooms, Vacation Bible schools, and even children's churches. But looking at this story from a different perspective allowed me to see several things. Jonah was outrightly disobedient to God. God told him to do something, and he adamantly put himself on a ship going in the opposite direction. He sleeps during a most harrowing storm and has to be woken by his shipmates. He confesses that the storm is after him and tells his shipmates to throw him over, but first they try to row to shore. Jonah is let off on the ground and not thrown over into the sea. But they realized you cannot outrun God when He is trying to get your attention.

Without even knowing him, his shipmates have great compassion for him. But Jonah was still disobedient to God. He still had work to do, and although he did not want to do it, he had to. God gave the assignment to him, and as long as he was still breathing, that assignment was his to complete. His choice to run did not change the assignment. It may have prolonged the completion, but the Lord was waiting.

Are there things the Lord is waiting for us to complete? Is the Lord patiently waiting as we run, making every excuse for why we cannot complete something He gave us to do?

Had I simply done what my father told me to do, I would not have gotten into trouble. But sometimes it takes getting into trouble you cannot get out of by yourself. Or even more, getting the help of someone who is compassionate or can show you mercy to help you out of that trouble.

What choices are you making with or without realizing you are heading in the wrong or opposite direction of what the Lord has called you to do?

Jonah considered the people of Nineveh evil, so he did not want them to repent and be blessed. He wanted them to die for their sins, but that was not for Jonah to decide but God. Jonah wanted their destruction, while God wanted to give them the opportunity to repent and live in the right choices and be blessed.

Do we ever think our decisions about people are right even when God wants to bring them to a better place? Our choice should be to obey God and allow His judgments to be by Him, not us, because the Lord could allow judgment on us the same way. Jonah's choice should have been to obey God and allow God to set in order everything else.

~ 7 ~

THE CONSECRATED THINGS OF THE LORD

Taking things that do not belong to you is something you may have to pay a heavy price for. Have you ever been in a store and saw a photo of someone who was banned for passing a bad check or stealing?

I was in Marshalls in 2018 doing some last-minute Christmas shopping with a couple of my grandchildren. We were in an aisle close to the entrance when I heard a lot of yelling and saw people running around. Two people had grabbed as many clothes as possible and were running toward the exit. Security personnel and one of the managers were right behind them, yelling for them to stop, which they didn't. A car was waiting right out front for them, so it was clearly planned and executed. The store manager was able to get the license plate number and called the police. While I don't know how this ended, I'm fairly sure it didn't go well for the thieves. It was unbelievable that it all happened in front of everyone shopping.

This story shows what happens when you take consecrated things that belong to God. We should not steal, but people do in times of desperation or even because that is what they want to do. I chose this story because in previous times, thieves faced a harsh punishment for themselves and their families, lessons that people watching would never forget.

In the stories we have looked at, all the people walked away with their lives. They may not have completely done what the Lord wanted initially, but they eventually did as He instructed and were blessed—except in this next account. There are some instructions from the Lord you never want to disobey, and this is one such anecdote.

It is the story of Achan, who is with Joshua when they march around Jericho, and the Lord gives them the city. On that seventh day, when the Israelites shouted and the walls fell, the Israelites were given instruction as to what was not clean and what was to be consecrated unto the Lord. Achan did not heed those instructions. The instruction of the Lord was to keep themselves from the accursed things. The gold, silver, vessels of brass, and iron were consecrated and were to go into the treasury of the Lord. Achan instead took the accursed things, and the Lord was angered with the children of Israel. Joshua and the others fighting alongside him did not know what happened until they went into the next battle and lost.

"But the children of Israel committed a trespass in the accursed thing: for Achan, the son of Carmi, the son of Zabdi, the son of Zerah, of the tribe of Judah, took of the accursed thing: and the anger of the Lord was kindled against the children of Israel."

Something that was supposed to be an easy victory cost them thirty-six men and to run from a battle they should have won. Joshua went before God and asked what happened. God told Joshua that Israel sinned and that they transgressed by taking the accursed things.

> And Joshua rent his clothes, and fell to the earth upon his face before the ark of the LORD until the eventide, he and the elders of Israel, and put dust upon their heads.
>
> And Joshua said, Alas, O Lord God, wherefore hast thou at all brought this people over Jordan, to deliver us into the hand of the Amorites, to destroy us? would to God we had been content, and dwelt on the other side Jordan! O Lord, what shall I say, when Israel turneth their backs before their enemies! For the Canaanites and all the inhabitants of the land shall hear of it, and shall environ us round, and cut off our name from the earth: and what wilt thou do unto thy great name?

> And the LORD said unto Joshua, Get thee up; wherefore liest thou thus upon thy face?
>
> Israel hath sinned, and they have also transgressed my covenant which I commanded them: for they have even taken of the accursed thing, and have also stolen, and dissembled also, and they have put it even among their own stuff. (Joshua 7:6–11)

This is grievous to Joshua, but he now has to figure out who did this. There are thirty thousand men and their wives and children with Joshua. God is telling Joshua there is a thief among them, and someone took things from a battle this person should not have touched.

God gives Joshua the strategy of how to find the person: break down the people by tribes, families, and households. Each man is questioned one by one. The Lord already told Joshua that whomever did this will be burnt with fire and all that he has. He could not destroy just the person; his entire family, servants, cattle, and all possessions were also destroyed because everything that person was associated with was considered part of the issue.

> And Joshua said unto Achan, My son, give, I pray thee, glory to the LORD God of Israel, and make confession unto him; and tell me now what thou hast done; hide it not from me. And Achan answered Joshua, and said, indeed I have sinned against the LORD God of Israel, and thus and thus have I done. (Joshua 7:19–20)

Achan was brought before Joshua and asked if he took the accursed things, and his reply was yes. He confessed that he sinned before Joshua and God. Joshua sent messengers to his tent to retrieve the accursed and consecrated things, who brought them out and lay them before Joshua and the Lord. Joshua asked why Achan had done this; he told Achan that the Lord would punish him for the trouble he caused Israel.

Achan, his wife, sons, daughters, oxen, cattle, sheep, and everything else they had were taken into the valley of Achor; all of Israel stoned them and burned them with fire. Achan and his entire family lost their lives on that day. His wife and children may not have known what he did, but the root of disobedience needed to be cut off, and God's judgment was swift.

When God gives instruction of what He wants His people to do, He expects His word to be followed. The statement "obedience is better than sacrifice" could not be more relevant here.

Achan heard the instruction and chose not to follow it. But in battle, there is always instruction for victory and a safe return. Though our battles are different, God still gives instructions that we need to take heed of for our victories. Are you obedient to God?

What would be the cost of your disobedience in any area? In being obedient to God, we must first count the cost of whatever we do for Him.

You may not lose your life today, but what if you lose your connection with God? What if death is spiritual? How do you call on God again for Him to hear you?

~ 8 ~

JOSEPH: THE LORD WAS WITH HIM

In this story, I wonder how Joseph felt when he went through all he did without his family around to guide him or talk to him. The story speaks that the Lord was with him. It had to still be difficult because he went through so much. The words "and the Lord was with him" seemed to give hope even if Joseph did not know God was there no matter what he went through. I chose this story because no matter what happened, there was still hope.

In going through my story, I did not always feel like it, but there was always hope. I may not have seen or looked in the right places, but even for me, the Lord was there.

Would you go through many harrowing things at a young age, potentially not seeing your family for many years knowing the outcome would be that one day you would be the second in charge of a nation? I'm not sure I would immediately sign up for that, but Joseph did not sign up for it either. It just happened. I love reading the story of Joseph and the multicolored coat.

More specifically, I love the story of how he went from prison to being second-in-command over Egypt. But there is so much more to the story. Joseph's choices led him to all the places he had to go through on his journey. When he had the dream where his brothers bowed to him and he decided to tell them about the dream, it was their anger toward him that led them to want to have him killed. His brothers were already jealous because every day, they would have to tend the sheep while Joseph was home. These were Joseph's half-brothers, and their father, Jacob, loved him and showed everyone around that he loved Joseph more than his brothers. Jacob made Joseph a coat of many colors, which was evident by the distinctions between this coat and the coats his brothers wore.

First and foremost, Joseph's coat had long sleeves. It came down almost ankle-length and was colorful. His brothers' coats were sleeveless; they stopped about mid-thigh and were more traditional in colors, such as brown or tan. Joseph's coat was one that someone with money or status in those days would have; his brothers' coats were not.

Joseph had two dreams. In the first dream, Joseph became lord over his brothers, and they bowed to him. In the second dream, his brothers and parents made obeisance to him, which made his brothers hate Joseph even more. His brothers went to feed their flock, and Jacob sent Joseph to check on his brothers and the flock. His brothers had moved the flock from one spot to another to ensure the flock had enough to eat. They saw Joseph coming from far off and plotted on how they would kill him.

But the oldest brother, Reuben, heard the plan and told them not to kill him but to throw him in a pit. Reuben left to go take care of other business for his father; his plan was to return and get Joseph out of the pit to return him to his father.

But after Reuben left, a company of Ishmaelites came from Gilead on their way to Egypt. The brothers decided to sell Joseph into slavery. When they went home, they took Joseph's coat, tore it into pieces, and dipped it in blood so Jacob would believe a beast devoured Joseph. Jacob mourned him.

In the meantime, Joseph was taken by the Midianites into Egypt to Potiphar, an officer of Pharaoh's, and captain of the guard. The Lord was with Joseph, and Potiphar put Joseph over all that he had. The Lord blessed Potiphar's house for Joseph's sake. Potiphar's wife became very attracted to Joseph and would try to lay with him, but Joseph would get away from her every chance he could. However, Potiphar's wife desired Joseph and tried to sleep with him.

One day Joseph came into the house to do his business. There were no other men in the house; Potiphar's wife tried to get Joseph to sleep with her again, and she grabbed him by his garment. Joseph left his garment in her hand. She called to the men of the house that Joseph came in to sleep with her and she told her husband. The captain (Potiphar's husband) put Joseph in prison. In those days, Joseph could have been put to death for attempting to sleep with his wife, but he was shown mercy. Joseph was favored while in prison; the Lord continued to be with him and made the things he did in prison prosper.

Let's look at a few things in Joseph's life that seem to be on a repeat cycle—not from Joseph, but the people around him. Joseph's brothers tried to kill his dream, so they would not bow to him. Joseph was betrayed by his brothers when they threw him into the pit and sold him into slavery; he was betrayed by Potiphar's wife when she tried to sleep with him. There was loss in Joseph's life; his mother died when he was young. If God was not with him, there are many things that could have happened to get Joseph to abandon his dream and who he was. Joseph's story does not end while in prison. Two new prisoners are brought in: the chief butler and the chief baker. They are put in where Joseph is bound, and both have a dream during their stay on the same night. Each dream causes the men to be sad, so they look for someone to interpret their dreams.
Joseph tells each man he will interpret them.

Within three days, it is Pharaoh's birthday, and he calls forth his chief baker and butler. As Joseph interpreted, Pharaoh hung the chief baker and restored the chief butler.

The one thing Joseph asked of each man was to remember him when they went back to the palace. That did not happen; not only did the chief butler not remember Joseph, he went about his life.

Two years later, Pharaoh had a dream that troubled him. He sent for his magicians and the wise men of Egypt to interpret the dream, but no one could. Then the chief butler spoke to Pharaoh about Joseph. Pharaoh called for Joseph to be brought forth immediately. Joseph had to be cleaned up, shaved, and his clothes changed in order to go before Pharaoh. When Joseph finally met with Pharaoh, he told Pharaoh God would give him an answer of peace.

Pharaoh told Joseph the dream, and God gave Joseph the interpretation. He also gave Pharaoh a strategy for what to do when the dream takes place to position the country so they will continue to grow. The dream was about seven years of prosperity, followed by seven years of drought (hardship). The strategy Joseph gave was that during the years of prosperity, the government should set aside food and bounty for the years of hardship so the people could come and get food.

Pharaoh was impressed with Joseph and made him second-in-command over the country. Pharaoh took off his ring and gave it to Joseph, gave him the best clothes, and put a gold chain around his neck.

Joseph was betrayed by the chief butler who said he would remember him when he was restored to his former position, but he didn't. I'm sure by then Joseph was beginning to feel discouraged, if he wasn't already. But God truly was with Joseph. All that he learned from being sold into slavery, being at Potiphar's house, and operating part of the prison prepared Joseph on how to run things effectively. He used all that he learned to provide the strategy and run the country.

A lot happened to Joseph from late teens to early adulthood. At age thirty he became second in charge. He had to have learned many lessons going through such hardships.

Like Joseph, through everything I went through, including all the stuff in law school, I still have hope. My hope and trust is in God.

~ 9 ~

FORGIVENESS

Forgiveness is a mature spiritual person's gift to themselves or someone else. It can be hard to forgive. I look at the story of Joseph and how much he had to grow to be in a position to forgive his brothers. From a young age, he went through so much in life without family members around and no one looking out for him but God. I realized I needed to forgive my classmate and myself.

Are there people in your life who have taken time for you to forgive or that it has been difficult to forgive? Even if the result of whatever it was that you went through turned out well, was it easy to forgive? Or did God work on your heart, understanding, and maturity in order for you to forgive?

Forgiveness gets easier with time. There have been times in my life where I had trouble forgiving people. I only looked at situations from one perspective. I would pray to God, asking why I should have to forgive when the people who hurt me walked away free to do whatever they want, and I struggled with the hurt and raw emotions that accompanied it. I didn't realize that forgiving freed me and allowed me the ability to move on.

It may not seem like it when you are initially going through that, but God gives you the strength and power to move forward, and eventually, the hurt is healed. You can move on. When you hold on to unforgiveness, you are doing yourself more harm than good because you are stuck in the hurt to relive it over and over again. Once you forgive, it becomes easier to let go.

How Did I Get Here? The Power of Choices

The story of Joseph does not end with him being elevated to the position of second in the country. We are now in the fulfillment of Pharaoh's dream, having had seven years of prosperity.

In contrast, God was with Joseph when he was thrown into the pit, sold into slavery, and imprisoned. God made the people's business prosper for the sake of Joseph. God ensured that Joseph would have a place to be no matter what he went through.

Now Joseph is second in command, and the famine has begun. His brothers come to buy grain so their family does not die. Joseph immediately recognizes his brothers, but they don't recognize him. He decides to invite them to have dinner at his house. While there, they gave him presents according to custom.

Joseph greeted his brothers and spoke to Benjamin, the youngest. He had to go into another room where he wept at seeing Benjamin because they both have the same mother. Once getting himself together and returning, he sat at his usual table, and his brothers sat at another table. Egyptians despise Hebrews and refuse to eat with them. They remained until morning with Joseph. He told his servant to put the money they brought back in each brother's bag. They also put Joseph's silver cup in it along with the money.

As they had traveled a bit, Joseph's servant caught up with them and searched each brother's bag from eldest to youngest. They found the silver cup in Benjamin's bag. Joseph told them to tell his brothers he could predict the future with that cup, and the brothers were brought back to Joseph's house. Judah asked to speak to Joseph privately, and he explained the difficulty in Jacob wanting Benjamin to go with the brothers to Egypt because another brother left to check on his brothers and never came back—so Judah said he would be Joseph's slave in Benjamin's place.

After a while, Joseph told his brothers who he was, and he wept so loudly that his servants heard him and asked his brothers if his father was still alive, to which they answered in the affirmative.

Joseph had told his brothers not to be troubled and that God sent him before them to preserve their lives. Joseph explained that the famine had only been going on for two years, and they still had five years left. He told them to gather their families, animals, belongings, and their father and bring them to Goshen. Pharaoh had given Joseph permission for Joseph's family to come and live in Egypt. Joseph would provide for them and their household for the next five years. Joseph's brothers were excited that he lived and that they would be moving their families to Goshen.

Jacob became sick and called his sons in to bless them. He asked Joseph to take him back and bury him in the land of Canaan. He wanted to be buried next to Rachel. Joseph asked Pharaoh for permission to bury his father, and it was granted. After the embalming and the time of mourning, Joseph and his brothers took Jacob to the land of Canaan to be buried.

Joseph and his brothers remained in Egypt, and he saw Ephraim's children for three generations. Before Joseph died, he told his brothers the Lord would visit and bring them out of the land of Egypt and into the land he swore to Abraham. Joseph took an oath to God regarding the children of Israel that they would carry his bones from Egypt. Joseph lived to be 110 years old.

Here are some things to think about. When Joseph was seventeen, he told his brothers about two dreams he had where they would bow to him, including his mother and father. Was Joseph bragging about what would happen? Maybe. His brothers became offended to the point they hated him enough to want to kill him. Each had a part at the beginning of the story where their positions and how they are perceived had to do with their reactions. They all had a level of immaturity over the situation. The dream came to pass. In Genesis 42–46, Joseph's brothers bowed to him over and over again. More importantly, he was in a position to be able to help his family more than anyone else.

By the time his brothers came to Egypt to buy wheat and other food, he had to have forgiven his brothers and be ready to help. He also had to understand his position and why the Lord put him there. He was a forerunner for the family. God's wisdom had to be in Joseph for him to provide the right answers to get him in the position of second in command, which was the only way to help his family.

What would you do in Joseph's position, knowing the anger and hatred his brothers had toward Joseph because of his dreams? Many years passed, so Joseph and his brothers had to be in a position to have forgiven each other or to forgive each other when Joseph revealed who he was. Was the outcome worth the process?

Sometimes we look at things from the wrong perspective. We look at the difficulties we face and are angered by the person we think is responsible instead of looking at the entire situation and being thankful that God brought us through without potentially receiving the punishment we justly deserve.

~ 10 ~

ESTHER: POSITIONED AT THE RIGHT TIME

The story of Esther reads a little like a fairy tale if you are only looking at it through the lens of her marrying the prince. It is so much more, and that is why I wanted to include it.

Esther had nothing to do with the circumstances that led to her getting the opportunity to be in a position to be chosen queen, but her life was set to ensure she had a chance. She was humble, diligent, educated, and knew protocol. If she was greedy or simply wanted to obtain wealth, she may not have ended up a queen.

Being in a position you have always wanted is a great achievement. But there are many lessons you need to learn along the way.

This story is about the process it took for Esther to become queen and go before the king. If Esther had not learned the process, she would not have lasted long in her duties as queen. The reason I chose this story is because in everything we go through there is a process. Whether we understand as we are going through or after, everything has a process.

In my home, I like to have kids ask to have water or juice, especially if they are young and can make a big mess trying to get it on their own. As my kids grew up and my grandkids came along, there was always a schedule that I kept to within the house. On weekdays I got up and walked our dog, Kiko, and then got ready for work. Sometimes I had a part-time job to go to or a class. These were the early years when I first bought my house.

How Did I Get Here? The Power of Choices

On weekends we cleaned, and Sunday was church. While this is not everything, it is a small part of the schedule. There were variations during holidays and the summer, but I needed structure. I preferred people knocking on the door instead of just walking in. Those were my protocols for my home. Other family members did not care if people walked into their home without knocking, especially if they knew you were coming.

My point is that how things are done in one place may not be how they are done in other places. You have to learn how things are done before asserting yourself into another's processes.

Ahasuerus (Xerxes) was king of Persia and Media. He made a feast for the people of Shushan in the palace for seven days, where he was showing the beauty and riches of the kingdom. On the seventh day before the seven chamberlains, he told the servers in the palace to bring Vashti, the queen, to him so the people and the princes could see her beauty. Queen Vashti was having her own royal feast and refused to come before the king. This infuriated him, which prompted him to ask an advisor, Memucan, what should be done to her. Memucan told Ahasuerus that other women would not do as their husbands told them once they heard of the queen's disrespect, and protocol said that she was to come before the king no more. In that instance, the kingdom no longer had a queen.

Ahasuerus was building his army and preparing for battle, but he could not leave Shushan without a royal on the throne during the time of war. Ahasuerus's advisors told him to round up all the virgins in the kingdom, give them beauty rituals, and prepare them to go before the king. These rituals took twelve months.

Meanwhile, a Jew by the name of Mordecai, who was raising his niece, Esther, was a scribe in the king's palace. Esther was one of the virgins to be gathered for the rituals. Esther found favor with Hegai, the keeper of women (Esther 2:8). The king loved Esther above all the women; she found favor and grace in his sight, and the king put the crown on Esther's head in place of Vashti.

The king had a man named Haman in his court. Haman was the son of Hammedatha the Agagite; he was set over all the princes of King Xerxes. Years earlier, Saul was sent by a prophet of God to kill all descendants of the Agagites, but Saul did not carry out God's decree. He left the queen to live, and she was pregnant. From those descendants who lived was a great hatred toward the Jewish people.

Haman was promoted to a prince in the king's court. He also set up a plot against the Jews who lived in Persia, Shushan, and throughout the region. He asked the king if a written decree could go out stating the Jews could be destroyed and all their possessions taken (their gold and silver were to be taken and brought back to be put in the king's treasury, and also their businesses if they had any). Haman's plot was presented to the king to raise money for the army.

Everything the Jewish people had would be taken from them, the Jewish people would be killed, and their money put into the king's treasuries. All this was to be done because the king was gathering finances to go to war. Letters went out, and when Mordecai saw what was to be done to the Jewish people, he tore his clothes in the king's gate as a sign of sadness. (The tearing of clothes was a sign of distress or deep sorrow before God.) Esther was told what happened and sent clothes for Mordecai to put on, but he refused. Mordecai sent word for Esther to go into the king's chamber to request that the Jews be spared. Esther sent word back that she had not been called to the king for thirty days and that she could not go into the king's inner court without the king summoning her.

> When Mordecai perceived all that was done, Mordecai rent his clothes, and put on sackcloth with ashes, and went out into the midst of the city, and cried with a loud and a bitter cry.
>
> And came even before the king's gate: for none might enter into the king's gate clothed with sackcloth. And in every province, whithersoever the king's commandment and his decree came, there was great mourning among the Jews, and fasting, and weeping, and wailing; and many lay in sackcloth and ashes.
>
> So Esther's maids and her chamberlains came and told it her. Then was the queen exceedingly grieved; and she sent raiment to clothe Mordecai, and to take away his sackcloth from him: but he received it not.

How Did I Get Here? The Power of Choices

Then called Esther for Hatach, one of the king's chamberlains, whom he had appointed to attend upon her, and gave him a commandment to Mordecai, to know what it was, and why it was.

So Hatach went forth to Mordecai unto the street of the city, which was before the king's gate. And Mordecai told him of all that had happened unto him, and of the sum of the money that Haman had promised to pay to the king's treasuries for the Jews, to destroy them.

Also he gave him the copy of the writing of the decree that was given at Shushan to destroy them, to shew it unto Esther, and to declare it unto her, and to charge her that she should go in unto the king, to make supplication unto him, and to make request before him for her people.

And Hatach came and told Esther the words of Mordecai. Again Esther spake unto Hatach, and gave him commandment unto Mordecai; all the king's servants, and the people of the king's provinces, do know, that whosoever, whether man or women, shall come unto the king into the inner court, who is not called, there is one law of his to put him to death, except such to whom the king shall hold out the golden scepter, that he may live: but I have not been called to come in unto the king these thirty days.

And they told to Mordecai Esther's words. Then Mordecai commanded to answer Esther, Think not with thyself that thou shalt escape in the king's house, more than all the Jews. For if thou altogether holdest thy peace at this time, then shall there enlargement and deliverance arise to the Jews from another place; but thou and thy father's house shall be destroyed: and who knoweth whether thou art come to the kingdom for such a time as this?

> Then Esther bade them return Mordecai this answer, Go, gather together all the Jews that are present in Shushan, and fast ye for me, and neither eat nor drink three days, night or day: I also and my maidens will fast likewise; and so will I go in unto the king, which is not according to the law: and if I perish, I perish. Mordecai went his way, and did according to all that Esther had commanded him. (Esther 4:1–17)

They fasted, and Esther put on royal clothes and went before the king. Just as the executioner was going to swing the sword at Esther, the king had favor with her and held out the golden scepter. Esther asked for a petition before the king.

Then the king said to her, "What do you wish, Queen Esther? What is your request? It shall be given to you—up to half the kingdom!" (Esther 5:3).

She asked if she could hold a banquet for the king and Haman. Through all this, Haman made gallows for the Jewish people to be hanged from.

One day the king could not sleep, and he had the book of records brought to him. He saw that Mordecai had saved his life and there was no recognition made to Mordecai. When he woke up the next day, he called Haman to his presence and asked what honor should be bestowed upon a man who saved the king's life.

Haman thought King Ahasuerus was talking about him, so he said, "Get a robe the king has worn and place it on him, put a ring the king has worn and put it on the man's finger, and let him ride through the town proclaiming that this man saved the king's life" (Esther 6:1).

The king thought those were good ideas and told Haman to do all he had spoken for Mordecai. Haman was angry because he thought the king wanted to do something for him.

Esther had the banquet set up for the king and Haman. The king asked Esther what her petition was and that she could have up to half his kingdom. Esther told him her people were in danger and were going to be destroyed. Furthermore, if they were not killed they were to be sold into slavery and made to be bondmen and bondwomen. The king asked who was out to destroy them, and Esther said it was Haman.

How Did I Get Here? The Power of Choices

Haman became afraid; the king stepped out into the garden. When the king came back, he saw Haman on the same bed as Queen Esther, and the king thought Haman was going to force himself on her. The king's guards grabbed Haman, and he was to be hanged on the gallows he built for Mordecai. It was not just Haman that was to be hanged but his entire family. A new decree was written; the decree from Haman to destroy the Jews was reversed and sealed with the king's ring.

The Jews in the kingdom and the provinces all around Shushan gathered and stood for their lives. They had rest from their enemies and defeated those who were trying to kill them. Mordecai wrote that the people should remember the day that would have been their destruction and celebrate because their enemies were defeated instead of them. Mordecai was celebrated because he wrote about everything and also wrote a decree to celebrate all that had happened. Mordecai was commemorated for being a Jew and next to the king.

In the book of Esther, we see how things are carried out and why certain things are done. Esther talks about protocol and that when the king makes a decree, it cannot be changed. We look at how a king looks to the people who surround him to give him counsel. There are times when Ahasuerus looks weak to those who surround him and how this can influence whether they stand strong with him or turn against him.

Esther was an orphan and a Jew in the land of the Gentiles. The time for the Jewish people to go back to Jerusalem after their captivity was over, but Mordecai stayed in Persia.

If you were to be elevated to a higher position and it's required to test whether you truly believe in God for your very life, what would you do? That is the position of Queen Esther and also, to a large extent, Queen Vashti. The reason Vashti did not want to come before the king was because the men had been drinking and partying for seven days. If it were you, what would you do? Vashti made a bad choice when she refused to come before the king. She may have thought she was protecting herself from being around all those partying drunk men, but she forgot about protocol. Queen Vashti forgot what she was throwing away by thinking her decisions were equal to the king's. She was wrong.

There may be a good reason for a bad decision, but sometimes it turns out to be the wrong decision. Vashti was the queen and had more than herself to think about in making some decisions. When the king asked what should be done, the decision was an easy one to make. Vashti broke protocol, and for that, the punishment was already in place.

How many times do we put ourselves in similar situations? We know what we should do, but we have reasons not to do it; however, in making that choice, you also agree to the consequences.

How many times do we know what the Lord wants us to do, but we reason our way out and make a decision that is based on principle? But the consequence of the decision is still in place, and we must accept that consequence. Also, the Lord always has a backup plan or substitute if we do not fulfill what He asks us to do. Esther was the substitute the Lord knew would fulfill all that was asked. She knew the law and the protocol of the kingdom. She risked death to go before Xerxes to plead for her life and the life of the Jews.

What is the Lord asking you to do? Will you do it? Are you positioned in the right place? And if you are not, will there be a substitute to take your place? There is nothing harder than watching someone else take your place.

~ 11 ~

GIDEON: IDENTITY CRISIS

Some things about the story of Gideon grabbed my attention. The cruelty of the Persians is one. The Persians were determined to starve the Israelites to death, but even Gideon hid to press wheat for food. Gideon determined even if his family and kin were all they had left they were going to eat the wheat Gideon pressed.

I chose this story because not knowing who you are or what you are supposed to do is a terrible thing. And Gideon is a perfect example. When you don't know who you are, you stand the chance of being abused because you allow others to treat you any kind of way.

When I first got to college, I had no idea what I wanted to major in. I was grateful to take general studies classes until I could figure it out. It was trial and error as I went to different groups to find out what the people were like. It showed me some of the majors I didn't want to be like or deal with. But It was not until my second semester that I knew I wanted to major in business. Even after that, it was a slow process to get to what I actually loved to do, which is contracts, and still part of business. Gideon fights mightily for God, but only after he is reminded of who he is and that God is with him. The first way Satan attacks the people of God is by having them wonder about their identity. Gideon asks God for many signs so that he knows God will be with him, and after those signs, he never forgets who he is.

It is easy to understand why Gideon was unsure of who he was because God was angry with the Israelites from the beginning of this story.

> The Israelites did evil in the Lord's sight. So the Lord handed them over to the Midianites for seven years. The Midianites were so cruel that the Israelites made hiding places for themselves in the mountains, caves and stronghold. Whenever the Israelites planted their crops, marauders from Midian, Amalek, and the people of the east would attack Israel, camping in the land and destroying crops as far away as Gaza. They left the Israelites with nothing to eat, taking all the sheep, goats, cattle and donkeys. These enemy hordes, coming with their livestock and tents were as thick as locusts; they arrived on droves of camels too numerous to count. And they stayed until the land was stripped bare. So Israel was reduced to starvation by the Midianites. Then the Israelites cried out to the Lord for help.
>
> When they cried out to the Lord because of the Midian's, the Lord sent a Prophet to the Israelites. He said, "This is what the Lord, the God of Israel, says: I brought you up out of slavery in Egypt. I rescued you from the Egyptians and from all who oppressed you. I drove out your enemies and gave you their land. I told you, 'I am the Lord your God. You must not worship the gods of the Amorites in whose land you now live.' But you have not listened to me." Then the angel of the Lord came and sat beneath the great tree at Ophrah, which belonged to Joash of the clan of Abiezer. Gideon son of Joash was threshing wheat at the bottom of a winepress to hide the grain from the Midianites. The angel of the Lord appeared to him and said, "Mighty hero, the Lord is with you!"
>
> "Sir," Gideon replied, "if the Lord is with us, why has all this happened to us? And where are all the miracles our ancestors told us about? Didn't they say,

'The Lord brought us up out of Egypt'? But now the Lord has abandoned us and handed us over to the Midianites." Then the Lord turned to him and said, "Go with the strength you have, and rescue Israel from the Midianites. I am sending you!"

"'But Lord,' Gideon replied, "how can I rescue Israel? My clan is the weakest in the whole tribe of Manasseh, and I am the least in my entire family!"

The Lord said to him, "I will be with you, and you will destroy the Midianites as if you were fighting against one man."

Gideon replied, "If you are truly going to help me, show me a sign to prove that it is really the Lord speaking to me. Don't go away until I come back and bring my offering to you."

He answered, "I will stay here until you return." (Judges 6:1–18 NLT).

I want to give you a little background of this story before we move forward. Since they would not listen to the Lord, they are in a situation where the Midianites are trying to starve them to death in their own land. Anytime something is planted and begins to grow, the Midianites come and take every last plant from the ground—not only the plants but the cattle, and all things to give them nourishment. The Midianites oppress the people so much they want to impoverish the people and destroy the land.

Gideon heard so many great stories of how the Lord helped his ancestors, but that doesn't seem to help with what they are going through. Until now, Gideon needs a sign to make sure the Lord is really talking to him. Gideon leaves and asks the angel of the Lord to stay so he can bring him an offering.

Gideon comes back and has cooked a young goat and baked bread without yeast and presents them to the angel of the Lord. The angel instructs Gideon to put the meat and bread on a rock and pour broth over them. The angel touches the rock with the tip of his staff, and fire flames up and consumes the broth, and the angel disappears. Gideon realizes he is talking to an angel of the Lord and thinks he will die because he has been face-to-face with him. The Lord speaks to Gideon and tells him not to be afraid; he will not die.

That night the Lord tells Gideon to get a bull from his father's herd—one that is seven years old—and pull down his father's altar to Baal. Finally, Gideon builds an altar to the Lord, lying the stones carefully and sacrificing the bull as a burnt offering on the altar, using the wood from the Asherah pole.

Gideon did all this at night, and the next morning when the people saw that the altar to Baal was broken down and the Asherah pole cut down, they started looking for who did it.

The people wanted to hurt Gideon for destroying them, but his father, Joash, asked the people, "Why are you defending Baal? If Baal is a god, let him defend himself."

From then on, Gideon was called Jerub-Baal, which means "Let Baal defend himself," because Gideon broke down Baal's altar.

Gideon was clothed with power from the Lord; he sent messages throughout Manasseh, Asher, Zebulun, and Naphtali calling for their warriors, to which they all responded, and Gideon asked for more signs from God.

As Gideon was approaching the Midian army, the Lord said he had too many warriors with him and told Gideon to tell the people that whomever is timid or afraid may leave the mountain and go home. Twenty-two thousand went home, and ten thousand remained to fight. The Lord said it was still too many, so He had Gideon bring the warriors to the water and divide them into two groups: the ones who drank from cupped hands and those who drank straight from the water. Only three hundred men drank with their hands, and the Lord told Gideon that those three hundred would give victory over the Midianites. He told Gideon to send the others home.

That night the Lord told Gideon to get up and go to the Midianite camp and listen to them to show they would have victory over the Midianites. Gideon went and listened to two men; one told the other about a dream he had, and then the other said the Lord had given Gideon, the Israelite, victory over Midian and all its allies. Once Gideon heard the interpretation of the dream, he left the camp and went back to his camp. Gideon was assured that he had victory over the Midianites.

How Did I Get Here? The Power of Choices

Gideon divided his army into three; each group had one hundred men. He gave each captain a ram's horn, and the men had jars to break. He told each to follow his lead once they were in position.

When they reached the edge of the Midianite camp, Gideon and the men blew their horns and broke their jars and shouted, "A sword for the Lord and for Gideon!"

The Midianites fought each other and then fled to places as far away as Beth-shittah near Zererah and to the border of Abel-meholah near Tabbath. Gideon sent for warriors of Naphtali, Asher, and Manasseh, and they joined the chasing of the army of Midian. Gideon also sent messengers throughout Ephraim to attack the Midianites and to cut them off in the shallow crossings of the Jordan River.

They captured Oreb and Zeeb—Midianite commanders— and killed them. The Israelites brought the heads of Oreb and Zeeb to Gideon. Gideon then crossed the Jordan River with his three hundred men, who by now were tired and hungry. They stopped at a town called Succoth, and Gideon asked for food for his warriors. The reply was they should catch Zebah and Zalmunna, the Midian kings, and then they would feed his army. It happened again in Peniel: Gideon asked for food for his warriors, and he received the same reply.

Gideon caught the two Midianite kings and all their warriors. Returning from battle, he captured a young man from Succoth and demanded he write down the names of all seventy- seven officials and elders in the town. He then took the elders and taught them a lesson by punishing them with thorns and briers from the wilderness. He also tore down the tower of Peniel and killed all the men.

After Gideon punished and killed the elders, he turned to Zebah and Zalmunna and asked if they remembered the men from Tabor that they killed. He told them the men killed were his brothers. Gideon told the kings he would not kill them if they had not killed his brothers. Zebah and Zalmunna told Gideon to be a man and kill them himself, so Gideon killed both kings and took the royal ornaments from them and their camels' necks.

The Israelites asked Gideon to be their ruler because he rescued them from the Midianites, but Gideon told them the Lord would rule over them. Gideon had one request from the warriors who took plunder—that each man gives him a gold earring. They did, and the weight of the gold earrings was forty-three pounds, not including the royal ornaments and pendants, the purple clothing worn by the kings of Midian, or the chains around the camels' necks.

Gideon returned home and had many wives and seventy sons. He also had a concubine in Shechem who gave birth to a son named Abimelech. After Gideon rescued the Israelites from the Midianites many years later he died when he was very old and buried in the grave of his father. The lesson is that the Israelites did not remember what Gideon did. After his death, the Israelites went back to worshipping the images of Baal and prostituted themselves before Baal. Furthermore, they went back to all they did before and forgot about Gideon rescuing them from the Midianites—and they forgot about God.

When the Lord's anger was against Israel and they were handed over to the Midianites for seven years, the conditions the Israelites found themselves in were terrible; the Midianites wanted to starve the Israelites. They prayed, and the Lord heard their prayers, but no one knew how the Lord would help. He chose Gideon because the Lord already knew who he was, even though Gideon did not. So when the angel of the Lord came, Gideon needed several signs.

Isn't that like our lives when we are not sure if the Lord is really talking to us or preparing us for something, and we do not know our own worth? Every time Gideon needed more reassurances, the Lord stepped in and gave him just that.

It is easy to abuse something when you don't know the value of it and even easier when it is a person who does not know his or her value.

Even when the angel of the Lord came to Gideon, he was not sure who he was. He stated, "I am the least in my clan," which is what he believed about himself.

The Midianites seemed to do whatever they wanted to the Israelites because they forgot who they were in God. After Gideon's death, they went back to worshipping Baal because there was no one to remind them of who they were in the Lord. I have seen a few books about the battlefield of the mind.

Once you are bombarded with negative situations and circumstances, it is easy to forget who you are in the Lord. Let us pray you never forget, and there is someone in your life who will always remind you.

Gideon realized who he is in God and became a mighty warrior. Finding out who you are can empower you to become more than you can ever imagine. It is becoming who God wants you to become.

CONCLUSION

For each story, including my own, I wanted to show why I chose it in this book and how the story I told had an effect on my life directly or indirectly. I am showing this so you may look at your life and examine yourself to make better decisions. In so many of these stories, the choice needed to be made, whether good or bad, which becomes life or death—or it at least appears to be. As believers, we are "killed all day long" by other people's tongues against us or by our own tongue, but our merciful God does not let that happen. But when we put ourselves in a position where death is truly laid in the balance, our prayer is that God will protect us. Put another way, walking toward death is no different than disobeying God's word because the wages of sin is death. It also answers the question,

"Have you sold out to God?"

We may say a lot of things in our efforts to make ourselves seem like great Christians; there is a time when God says, "Show me." So we must.

There are so many more stories in the Bible that I could have illustrated, but I wanted to give some examples of who made choices and how those choices affected them.

One character in the Bible I didn't talk about was Jesus Christ of Nazareth. He had many choices, and every choice He made lined up with what He came to do on earth. At age twelve, when He went to the temple and His parents were looking for him for days, Jesus asked them parents, "Didn't you know I would be doing the Lord's work?" (Luke 2:49).

When He was baptized, the Lord said, "This is my beloved Son, in whom I am well pleased" (Matthew 3:17).

And when He performed His first miracle of turning water into wine, it was the start of his public ministry, but it was still doing the things His Father taught Him to do (John 2:6–10).

In John, Jesus says, "I say or do nothing of myself but everything the Father says for me to do" (John 5:19; 12:49; 5:30; 8:28).

Jesus never forgot that He was here to do what His father sent Him to do. The words spoken and His actions were what His father wanted once He was in his public ministry. Let us never forget who we are in Christ Jesus.

We need to make intentional choices out of wisdom in order to get to our destinies. For some, time is simply a measure of a day. For those in the kingdom, it's about how long we have to work for Christ before night comes and we can no longer work. "I must work the works of him that sent me, while it is day:

the night cometh, when no man can work" (John 9:4).

Pray this prayer: Heavenly Father, thank You for protecting me from things seen and unseen. Help me forgive others who

have wronged me knowingly and unknowingly. Help me make the right choices lined up with Your will for my life and destiny. Send people into my life to remind me of who I am in You and to give me encouragement no matter what I go through. And I thank You and praise You for all You have allowed me to do in Your kingdom. Amen.